The Initiation

by Abu Laith As-Samarqandi

The Initiation

by Abu Laith As-Samarqandi:
A primer in the Hanafi School of jurisprudence.

Translated by Arfan Shah
with permission and supervision from
Sheikh Atabek Shukurov

Published by Islamic Information Society

ISBN 978 1 907888 00 7

Published by Islamic Information Society
www.isinsoc.org

4

CONTENTS

Introduction	11
1. Chapter expounding on the obligation of prayer	13
2. Chapter expounding on the types of obligation	17
3. Chapter on the benefits of prayer	17
4. Chapter on the kinds of impurity	19
5. Chapter on the kinds of purity	19
6. Chapter on the kinds of water	21
7. Chapter on the actions of prayer	25
8. Chapter on the proofs for the pillars of the prayer	27
9. Chapter on the obligations of prayer	33
10. Chapter on the Sunnas of the prayer	35
11. Chapter on the forgetful prostration	37
12. Chapter on ablution	39
13. Chapter on the Sunnas of ablution	41
14. Chapter on the supererogatory (Nawafil) acts of ablution	41
15. Chapter on the desired (Mustahab) acts of ablution	43
16. Chapter on the etiquette (Adab) of ablution	43
17. Chapter on the disliked actions of ablution	45
18. Chapter on the prohibitions of ablution	45
19. Chapter on the kinds of Istinja	47
20. Chapter on the number of what you can do Istinja with	49
21. Chapter on what is permissible to do Istinja with	51
22. Chapter on what is prohibited to use for Istinja	51
23. Chapter on the definition and meaning of Istinja, Istinqa and Istibraa	53
24. Chapter on the requirement of the Mustanji	55
25. Chapter on the description of ablution	57
26. Chapter on the kinds of purification	61
27. Chapter on the types of cleanliness	63
28. Chapter on the kinds of Sunna	63
29. Chapter on different issues	65

Introduction

All praise is for Allah; the Creator of all things; the One who sends mercy even though we are not worthy of it; the One who blessed us with the religion of Islam even though we are heedless; the One who gave mankind the ability to understand; and may infinite blessings be upon His final Messenger Muhammad (may Allah bestow upon him peace and blessings).

This is an introductory text to the Hanafi School of jurisprudence. This is the work of the great Hanafi scholar, Abu Laith As-Samarqandi, born in modern day Uzbekistan, and it seems fitting that a renowned scholar of that community, Sheikh Atabek, found this lost text and is allowing us to benefit from it. This text covers prayer and ablution, and all the issues pertaining to these actions, as well as some additional questions. We are now presenting you the translation of this text. A more detailed commentary on this text is also underway and will be available soon, Insha-Allah

To truly benefit from this text it needs to be studied with a teacher of the Hanafi School. Although reading through the text will, without doubt, bring some benefit, the true understanding of this text will only come with a teacher.

We pray that Allah (Mighty and Majestic) accepts this from us, His unworthy servants. We pray that the text benefits whoever reads it, and may Allah bless Abu Laith for writing such a wonderful text. Finally we would like to thank Nabila Rogob for proof reading the work.

The text was translated by Arfan Shah.

In the name of Allah,
The Most Compassionate,
The Most Merciful

'The Initiation' by the Jurist Abu Laith As-Samarqandi

1. Chapter expounding on the obligation of prayer

All praise is rightfully for Allah, Lord of the universe. The best endings are for the pious and there is no retribution except upon the oppressors. Peace and blessings upon the Best of Creation, Muhammad (may Allah bestow upon him peace and blessings), his family and his companions. The jurist, Abu Laith As-Samarqandi (may Allah show him mercy) said, Know that prayer is a continuous obligation, soundly established by the Sacred Law. Its injunction is known through the Quran, the Sunna and by the consensus of the scholars.

Allah states in the Quran, **"Establish worship and pay the tax."**[1] Allah (Mighty and Majestic) orders us to perform the prayer and pay the tax, and an order from Allah indicates compulsion. Also, **"Be guardians of your prayers and especially of the midmost prayer and stand up with devotion to Allah."**[2]

---

[1] Quran: The Heffer 2:110.
[2] Quran: The Heffer 2:238.

Meaning, be dedicated to Allah (Mighty and Majestic), He has ordered us to maintain the five daily prayers, and an order from Allah the Exalted indicates necessity. The Quran states, **"Worship at fixed times has been enjoined on the believers."[1]** Meaning, appointed times for obligatory prayers.

From the Hadith, it is related from Abdullah Ibn Umar[2] and Jabir Ibn Abdullah Al-Bujali[3] (may Allah be pleased with them) that the Prophet (may Allah bestow upon him peace and blessings) said, *"Islam is built on five; testifying that there is no deity except Allah and Muhammad is his servant and messenger, establishing prayer, paying alms, fasting during the month of Ramadan and performing Hajj for whoever is able to do so."[4]*

Elsewhere, in another narration, the Prophet (may Allah bestow upon him peace and blessings) said at the farewell sermon, *"O' People, pray your obligatory prayers, fast your month, go to the house of your Lord, give alms from your wealth in the best way from yourselves, and enter Heaven without reckoning or punishment."[5]*

The Prophet (may Allah bestow upon him peace and blessings) said, *"Prayer is a pillar of the religion. Whoever establishes*

---

[1] Quran: The Women 4:103.

[2] Abdullah Ibn Umar (Prince of the believers) Ibn Al-Khattab, embraced Islam with his father during childhood and migrated (to Medina) before his father. He passed away in 73 Hijri when he was 86 years old. He was born one year before the revelation. (Isad Al-Ghabah).

[3] Jahir Ibn Abdullah Ibn Jahir Al-Bujali embraced Islam forty days before the passing away of the Prophet (peace and blessing be upon him). He was a leader of his people. He passed away in 51 Hijra. (Isad Al-Ghabah).

[4] Bukhari and Muslim.

[5] Imam Ahmad and At-Tirmidhi from Abdullah Ibn Umar.

it, has established the religion. Whoever has left it, has destroyed the religion."[1]

This is the consensus of scholars from the time of the Prophet (may Allah bestow upon him peace and blessings) to our time concerning the obligation of prayer and alms, without rejecter or rejection.

The consensus of the scholars is from strong proofs and from that which is narrated from the Prophet (may Allah bestow upon him peace and blessings) who said, *"My nation will not unanimously agree to an error."*[2]

---

[1] Bayhaqi in Shu'ab al-Iman from Umar.

[2] Tabarani in Mu'jam al Kabir.

2. Chapter expounding on the types of obligation

Know that obligations are of two types:

1. Individual obligation
2. Collective obligation.

The individual obligation is that which, if some perform it, doesn't fall from the remainder, like fasting, prayer, alms, Hajj, ablution for prayer, washing from major impurity, periods, postpartum bleeding and war, if there is a general call to arms.

Collective obligation, if performed by some, it falls from the remainder. For example, return greeting, replying to a sneeze, visiting the sick, attending funeral prayer, prayer on the Prophet (may Allah bestow upon him peace and blessings), commanding good and prohibiting evil and war, if there isn't a general call to arms.

3. Chapter on the benefits of prayer

Know that prayer brings mercy and forgiveness from Allah the Exalted, His angels seek forgiveness for you, and the believers supplicate. In language, supplication is an expression, and in legal terms, is from the well known pillars of definite actions.

4. Chapter on the kinds of impurity

Know that impurity is of two types:

1. Actual impurity
2. False Impurity.

Actual impurity is urine, faeces, nosebleed, blood etc. False impurity is sleep, unconsciousness, insanity and laughing out loud in every prayer with a prostration and bowing.

5. Chapter on the kinds of purity

Know that purity is of two kinds:

1. Major purity
2. Minor purity.

Major purity is bathing, after one becomes **impure** from a major impurity,[1] periods and postpartum bleeding.[2] Minor purity is ablution.

---

[1] For example, after relations with spouse.
[2] After child-birth.

6. Chapter on the kinds of water

Know that water is of two kinds:

1. Absolute water
2. Restricted water.

Absolute water is all water that if you looked into it, would resemble absolute water like rain, spring, well, sea, pond and pool water etc. The ruling is that it is pure as long as it is free from actual impurity and false impurity from the body or clothes. Then it is permissible to use for ablution or ritual bathing.

Restricted water is all water that comes from acting on something like cucumber, pumpkin, watermelon and so forth. The ruling is that it is pure but not purifying from actual filth from the clothes or body. It is not permissible to do ablution or ritual bathing with. This is mentioned in the abridgement of the book Al-Karkhi[1] and Tahawi[2] in his book and this is the soundest opinion.

---

[1] Abaidullah Ibn Al-Hussain Ibn Dallal Al Karkhi was a teacher of Imam Abu Bakr Al-Razi Al-Jisas, writer of Quranic Exegesis, Abu Abdullah Ad-Damaghni, Abu Ali Al-Shahsi, writer of the principles/Usul As-Shahsi. He passed away in 340 Hijra. (Taj Al-Tarajim, Jawahir Mudiah).

[2] Ahmed Ibn Muhammad Ibn Salama Al-Azdi (Abu Jafar Al-Tahawai) Al-Faqi Al-Muhadith Al-Hafid. He taught Ibn Muzfar Al-Baghdadi Al-Hafiz, Abu Kasim Al-Tabarani, writer of the Al-Muajam and others. He was an outstanding trustworthy Hadith narrator. Ahmed passed away in 321 Hijri (Taj Al-Tarajim).

Muhammad Ibn Hasan[1] said that pure water that is not purifying, doesn't remove actual filth or false filth from clothes or body and it is not permissible to bathe or do ablution with. This is the opinion of Zufar and Imam Shafi[2] (may Allah show them mercy). Abu Laith mentions in *Differences* and in his other book *The Springs* that actual filth is not removed and neither is false filth from the body, in all their opinions. The only difference is in clothes; it does with Abu Hanifa and Abu Yusuf, but not with Imam Muhammad, and this is the opinion of Zufar and Shafi.

Imam Muhammad mentions the same issue as was in Al-Karkhi and Tahawi, and this is as they said. Abu Yusuf[3] (may Allah show him mercy) mentioned this in *Amali*, that all clothes, when actual filth is on them, the ruling is that what is wrung out

---

[1] Abu Abdullah Muhammad Ibn al Hassan Al Shayibani was a student of Abu Hanifa in jurisprudence and was from a village in Khurasan. He taught Imam Al-Mutalbi Muhammad Ibn Idrees As-Shafi, Abu Ubayd Al-Qasim Ibn Salam, Ibn Muyan and others. He was a narrator of the "Six books of jurisprudence" and passed away in 237 Hijra.

[2] Muhammad Ibn Idress Ibn Al-Abbas Ibn Uthman Ibn As-Shafi. He is from the tribe Al-Muttalib, Quresh and he is one of the four founders of the Madhabs and was born in the year 150. Imam Ahmed said, "There is no one who used paper and an inkpot of any superiority, except that Al Shafi took from him." His Madhab/School spread in Hijaz and Iraq and when he moved to Egypt, (199 Hijra) there also. He passed away in 204 and authored the following, "Al-Umm" in jurisprudence, "Al-Risala" in principles of Jurisprudence, and "Ahkam ul-Quran."

[3] Yaqoub Ibn Ibrahim Al-Qadi, was one of biggest students of Abu Hanifa. He was the first one to collect the principles of jurisprudence, except his works did not reach us. He passed away in 181.

by wringing removes filth , for example milk and vinegar. Everything that is not wrung out by (the process of) wringing, will not remove filth, like honey, butter, fat, treacle etc.[1]

---

[1] These all do not remove actual filth.

7. Chapter on the actions of prayer

Know that prayer has conditions, pillars, requirements, Sunnas, and etiquettes to fulfil the validity and legality of the prayer, free from the disliked and forbidden.

The conditions are six:
1. Cleanliness from impurity
2. Cleanliness from filth
3. Lack of nakedness
4. Facing the Qibla
5. Time
6. Intention.

The pillars are six:
1. Opening magnification
2. Standing
3. Recitation
4. Bowing
5. Prostration
6. Sitting in the final unit and reciting the Tashahud.

Leaving the prayer with the action of the prayer is an obligation with Abu Hanifa (may Allah show him mercy). This is not a condition for Abu Yusuf and Imam Muhammad. Know that the opening magnification is not part of the prayer according to Abu Hanifa, however, for Abu Yusuf and Imam Muhammad (may Allah show them mercy) it is.

8. Chapter on the proofs for the pillars of the prayer

We say that cleanliness from all filth is a condition proved by the Quran and Hadith. The Quran states, **"O' you who believe! When you rise up for prayer, wash your faces, and your hands up to the elbow, and lightly wipe your heads and wash your feet up to the ankles."**[1]

Allah (Mighty and Majestic) ordered us to wash three limbs, wipe the head, and an order from Allah (Mighty and Majestic) makes it an obligation.

Hadith: It is related that the Prophet (may Allah bestow upon him peace and blessings) said, *"Everything has a key and the key to prayer is cleanliness. The entrance is magnification and the exit is greeting."*[2]

We say that cleanliness from major filth is a condition by the Quran and the hadith, The Quran states, **"Thy raiment purify."**[3] The exegesis on this verse means to shorten.[4]

Hadith: the Prophet (may Allah bestow upon him peace and blessings) said, *"Allah does not accept prayer without*

---

[1] Quran: The Table Spread 5:6.

[2] Al-Hakim from Abu Said Al-Khudri, At-Tirmidhi and Abu Dawood from Ali.

[3] Quran: Divorce 65:4.

[4] Shorten one's clothes.

cleanliness, and charity from theft."[1] Theft is stolen spoils of war. We say that the place must be purified and so on.

We say that to cover nakedness is a condition of the prayer by the Quran and the Hadith. The Quran states, **"O children of Adam! Look to your adornment at every place of worship."**[2] The purpose of this is to adorn.

Hadith: Abu Hurayrah[3] (may Allah be pleased with him) narrates that the Prophet (may Allah bestow upon him peace and blessings) was asked about praying in one garment, to which he replied *"Or can you not find two garments?"* Or in another narration, *"Everyone use two garments."*[4]

We say that facing the Qibla is a condition of the prayer by the Quran and the Hadith. Quran: **"So turn thy face to the**

---

[1] Muslim from Ibn Umar.

[2] Quran: the Heights 7:31.

[3] Abu Hurayrah Abdurrahman Ibn Shkhir Ad-Dausi, companion of the Prophet (peace and blessings be upon him) narrated the most hadith. He said, "During the times of ignorance, my name was Abdus-shams then the Prophet (peace and blessings be upon him) named me Abdurrahman. I was called Abu Hurayrah because I used to keep a kitten up my sleeve. Then someone said to me", "You are Abu Hurayrah."(You are father of cats!) He passed away in 59 Hijri when he was 78 years old. (Isad Al-Ghabah).

[4] Bukhari and Muslim from Abu Hurayrah.

28

inviolable place of worship (Ka'ba) and whosesoever you may be turn your faces toward it."[1]

Hadith: It is narrated the Prophet (may Allah bestow upon him peace and blessings) taught a Bedouin the pillars of prayer and instructed him to face the Qibla.

We say that time is a condition by the Quran and Hadith. Quran: Allah (Mighty and Majestic) states, **"So glorify Allah when you enter the night, when you enter the morning. Unto Him be praise in the heavens and in the earth – and at the sun's decline and in the noonday."**[2] This refers to the times of the prayers as it is mentioned in exegesis.

Hadith: It is narrated that the Prophet (may Allah bestow upon him peace and blessings) said, *"I was ordered by Gibril, upon him peace, to face the Ka'ba for two days, then firstly he prayed Fajr at first light, secondly he prayed Zuhur after the sun passed the zenith, prayed Asr when the shadow of everything reached a like amount of its length minus the shadow at the zenith, prayed Maghrib after sunset and Isha after the redness left the sky."* Twilight is the whiteness that is across the horizon after redness according to Abu Hanifa. Abu Yusuf, Muhammad, and Imam Shafi say it is the redness. He prayed Fajr at sunrise and Zuhur when the shadow of everything is like it. He prayed Asr when the shadow of everything is twice its length of its height minus the shadow at the zenith. Prayed

---

[1] Quran: The Heffer 2:144.
[2] Quran: The Romans 30:114.

Maghrib when the faster breaks his fast and prayed Isha when a third of the night has passed. *Then he turned to him and said, "O Muhammad, these are your times and the times of the Prophets before you and the time of your nation is between the two."*[1]

Surely, we say that intention is a condition by the Quran and Hadith. Allah says in the Quran: **"And they are ordered naught else than to serve Allah, keeping religion pure for him."**[2] Sincerity will not be reached except by intention and intention is the goal.

Hadith: It is narrated that the Prophet (may Allah bestow upon him peace and blessings) said, *"Actions are commensurate to intentions, to every intender is his intention. Whoever's emigration is for Allah and his Messenger, then his emigration is to Allah and his Messenger. And whoever's emigration is for any worldly gain or for a woman he is to wed, then his emigration is for what he migrated."*[3]

Truly, we say that the opening magnification is a pillar by the Quran and the Hadith. Allah says in the Quran: **"And mention the name of your Lord then pray."**[4] Also, **"Thy Lord magnify."**[5]

---

[1] At-Tirmidhi, Imam Ahmad and Bayhaqi from Ibn Abbas.
[2] Quran: The Fig 98:5.
[3] Bukhari and Muslim from Umar.
[4] Quran: The Most High 87:15.
[5] Quran: the cloaked one 74:3.

Hadith: It is narrated that the Prophet (may Allah bestow upon him peace and blessings) said, *"The key to prayer is purification, its entrance is magnification and its exit is greeting."*[1]

Truly, we say that standing is a pillar by the Quran and Hadith. Allah states in the Quran, **"Stand up with devotion to Allah."**[2] The meaning is dedication.

Hadith: The Prophet (may Allah bestow upon him peace and blessings) said, *"The prayer of the sick is standing, if you are unable, sitting. If you are unable, lying down on your back indicating with your head. If you are unable, postpone your prayer, as Allah (Mighty and Majestic) is the first to forgive."*[3]

Truly, we say that recitation is a pillar by the Quran and the Hadith. Allah says in the Quran: **"Recite then what is easy from the Quran."**[4]

Hadith: The Prophet (may Allah bestow upon him peace and blessings) said, *"There is no prayer except with Sura Fatiha."*[5] Meaning, recitation.

---

[1] Al-Hakim from Abu Said Al-Khudri, At-Tirmidhi and Abu Dawood from Ali.

[2] Quran: The Heffer 2:238.

[3] Bayhaqi in As-Sughra 1/621 and Tabarani in Mu'jam Al-Awsat 4/3997 from Ali.

[4] Quran: The Enshrouded One 73.20.

[5] At-Tirmidhi 2/247, Ibn Hibban 5/1786 and Abu Awana 1/1664-1665 from Ubada.

Truly, we say that bowing and prostrating is a pillar by the Quran and Hadith. Allah says in the Quran: **"O' you who believe! Bow down, prostrate yourselves, worship your Lord, and do good."**[1]

Hadith: It is narrated that the Prophet (may Allah bestow upon him peace and blessings) taught a Bedouin the pillars of prayer that included bowing and prostration.

We truly say that the final sitting is a pillar by the Quran and the Hadith. Allah says in the Quran: **"Those who remember Allah standing, sitting and on their sides."**[2]

Hadith: It is narrated that the Prophet (may Allah bestow upon him peace and blessings) said, *"If you did as the Imam until the final sitting, then the prayer is complete; likewise the followers, if their state was like the Imam's."*[3]

---

[1] Quran: The Hajj 22.77.
[2] Quran: The Family of Imran 3.191.
[3] Not found currently.

9. Chapter on the obligations of prayer

The obligations are seven:

1. To recite Sura Fatiha
2. And a Sura with it or something from the Quran, in the first two units
3. The first sitting
4. Reading the Tashahud in the final sitting
5. Supplication in the Witr prayer
6. Pillars in order
7. Reciting aloud in aloud prayers and silently in the remainder.

The first group says the above are obligations, whilst the second group says that these are Sunna.[1]

The differences about the forgetful prostration: if left intentionally, then the forgetful prostration is not obligatory by agreement but if left forgetfully, the first group says that it is necessary while other says it is not necessary.[2]

---

[1] In reference to the above points.
[2] This is a reliable position and please see further discussion in section on forgetful prostration.

10. Chapter on the Sunnas of the prayer

The Sunnas are twelve:

1. Raising hands to the earlobes
2. Putting the right hand over the left under the belly button
3. Thana (or beginning supplication)
4. Seeking refuge from satan
5. Saying: Bismillah
6. Saying: Ameen
7. Saying: Allah hears who praises Him
8. Saying: To our Lord is praise
9. Glorification of Allah during bowing and prostrating
10. Reading Tashahud in the final sitting
11. Reading Sura Fatiha in the final two units of a four unit prayer
12. Magnification[1] in prayer during it except the first magnification.

Saying the greeting, and all other things, are etiquettes and should not be left.

---

[1] Say Allah is the Greatest/Allahu Akbar.

11. Chapter on the forgetful prostration

So, if something is left from what we call a condition then the prayer is invalid, even if left unintentionally or forgetfully.

If something that we call a pillar is left, then it has to be repeated, and if a repetition is not possible, then the prayer is invalid.

If something is left from what we call obligation and done forgetfully, then they have to perform the forgetful prostration, but the prayer is weak and incomplete.[1]

If something we call Sunna is left, there is no forgetful prostration, if done forgetfully or unintentionally.

---

[1] It remains weak if the forgetful prostration is not done, but when done it makes up for the error. If it is not done at all then they have to repeat the prayer in its time according to a reliable position and, according to the scholars of the Indo-Pak subcontinent, they have to repeat regardless of time.

12. Chapter on ablution

Know that ablution has (acts of) obligation, Sunna, supererogatory, desired, etiquette, disliked and prohibitions.

The obligations are four:

1. Washing the face: the face is what a person will see when they look towards you, beginning from the hairline to below the chin and from earlobe to earlobe. The skin between the ear and beard is to be washed according to Abu Hanifa and Imam Muhammad (may Allah show them mercy), but not with Abu Yusuf and Imam Shafi

2. Washing the hands up to the elbows

3. Wiping the head

4. Washing the feet up to the ankles, and the proof from the Quran, **"O' you who believe! When ye rise up for prayer, wash your faces, and your hands up to the elbows, and lightly rub your heads and wash your feet up to the ankles."**[1] Allah (Mighty and Majestic) has ordered us to wash three limbs, wipe the head, and an order from Allah the Exalted indicates to it obligation. The ankles and the elbow bone have to be washed according to our scholars except Zufar.

---

[1] Quran: The Table Spread 5:6.

13. Chapter on the Sunnas of ablution

The Sunnas of ablution are ten:
1. Saying Bismillah in the beginning of the ablution
2. Washing hands before putting hand into container
3. Istinja with water, when it's available, or stone or clay if unavailable
4. Miswak
5. Rinsing mouth
6. Cleaning nose
7. Wiping ears
8. Takheel the beard
9. Takheel the fingers
10. Washing the parts of the body for a second time.

14. Chapter on the supererogatory (Nawafil) acts of ablution

The supererogatory actions of the ablution are six:
1. Wiping hands on a wall or earth after Istinja
2. Washing the hands after wiping on the wall or earth
3. Mentioning a supplication when washing each limb
4. Wiping the back of the neck
5. Splashing water on the private place or underwear after completing ablution
6. Washing each limb three times

15. Chapter on the desired (Mustahab[1]) acts of ablution

The desired acts of ablution are six:
    1. Intention when beginning ablution
    2. Beginning by mentioning Allah
    3. Beginning with right side
    4. Maintaining order
    5. Following one limb after the other before they dry
    6. Wiping the entire head.

16. Chapter on the etiquette (Adab)[2] of ablution

The etiquettes of ablution are six:
    1. Don't face the Qibla or have your back to it
    2. Don't face the sun or moon or have your back to them
    3. Do not speak except supplication which you are saying when washing that limb
    4. Putting water into mouth and nose with right hand
    5. Blowing water from the nose with the left hand
    6. Covering nakedness after Istinja.

---

[1] Some of the scholars used to differentiate between Nafl and Mustahab but the most reliable opinion is that there is no difference.

[2] There is not a lot of difference between Mustahab and Adab, but Adab has lesser degree than Mustahab.

17. Chapter on the disliked actions of ablution

The disliked actions are six:
1. Striking your face with water
2. Looking at your private place
3. Releasing spit or snot into the water
4. Rinsing the mouth
5. Cleaning the nose with the right hand without excuse
6. Speaking when washing private places.

18. Chapter on the prohibitions of ablution

The Prohibitions of the prayer are six:
1. Uncovering nakedness after Istinja
2. Urinating or defecting in water for cleaning
3. Doing Istinja with right hand without excuse
4. Wasting water in ablution and ritual bath
5. Washing the mentioned limbs more than three times or less than three times.
6. Wiping the uncovered feet is prohibited, it is highly prohibited to wipe the feet, and the prayer is not valid with this ablution.[1]

---

[1] To wipe instead of washing, as the Shia wipe their feet not wash, therefore their ablution is not valid if one wipes bare feet.

19. Chapter on the kinds of Istinja

Know that Istinja is of nine kinds, four are obligatory, one is necessary, one is Sunna, one is desired, one is precautionary and one is innovation.

The four that are obligatory they are:

1. Istinja after relations with partner
2. Periods
3. Postpartum bleeding
4. If filth of more than the amount of a two-pound coin[1] is on you, then it is necessary to remove it.

The obligatory ablution: When filth is the amount of a two-pound coin, to remove it is necessary.

Sunna: If the filth is less than the amount of a two-pound coin, then it is Sunna to remove it.

Desired: If urinated, not defecated, then wash the private place and not the anal passage.

---

[1] Or the common explanation is the amount of water left in a normal hand if the water is gathered on the palm.

Precautionary: If something came out of the body and did not spread, then you only have to clean that place.

Innovation: If nothing came out of both passages except for wind from the rear. Then it is an innovation to wash it (the rear).

20. Chapter on the number of what you can do Istinja with

To do Istinja with three stones, pebbles or three handfuls of dust, is acceptable by our scholars, may Allah have mercy on them. Cleanliness is a condition, but the number is not. So if you do Istinja with one stone with three sides, and use each side once until you are clean, then it is permissible with us. The number is a condition with Imam Shafi (may Allah the Exalted show him mercy). Ibn Masud[1] (may Allah be pleased with him) related that he was with the Prophet (may Allah bestow upon him peace and blessings) when he met the Jinn and asked me for some stones for Istinja. So I brought two stones and piece of faeces. He (may Allah bestow upon him peace and blessings) threw away the faeces and said, *"This is filth, nakas."*[2] Nakas and filth carry the same meaning.

We say this Hadith is the proof because the Prophet (may Allah bestow upon him peace and blessings) took two stones and threw the faeces away. If number were a condition then he (may Allah bestow upon him peace and blessings) would have asked

---

[1] Abdullah Ibn Masud Ibn Gafil Abu Abdulrahim Al-Hazi was amongst the first Muslims. He was like a servant to the Prophet (may Allah bestow upon him peace and blessings) because of his love. He used to help him put on his shoes, he would walk in front of him, cover him if he washed, wake him if he was asleep and he used keep the siwak for him. He was seen in heaven with the Prophet (may Allah bestow upon him peace and blessings). He passed away in 32 Hijri, Medina and was in his 60s when he passed away.

[2] Bukhari.

for a third. So when he did not ask for a third, then this proves that number is not a condition but cleanliness is. If you can clean with one stone then you don't need to use two, if you can't, use three. If you are not clean by three then use more until you are clean.

21. Chapter on what is permissible to do Istinja with

It is permissible to Istinja with six things:

1. Stones
2. Clay
3. Dust
4. Old clothes
5. Sun-baked brick
6. Cotton etc.

22. Chapter on what is prohibited to use for Istinja

It is disliked to do Istinja with:

1. Bone
2. Dung
3. Clay pots
4. Tiles
5. Animal food and so on

23. Chapter on the definition and meaning of Istinja, Istinqa and Istibraa

Question: "What is the difference between Istinja, Istinqa and Istibraa?" Reply: "Istinja is using water or stones to clean oneself."

What is Istinqa? This is a desire for cleanliness by using stones, clay or other than that. Some say: "It is to wipe the place of defecation until the smell goes, with the hand." Some say to dry with a towel or cloth so that no used water drips onto you.

Istibraa: Is when a man coughs until urine is fully removed from himself. Others say that he should move away from the toilet, to a clean place and stamp his feet until he is sure that there is no urine left inside him.

24. Chapter on the requirement of the Mustanji

Know that the Mustanji (the one who is cleaning themselves) has essentials when entering and leaving the toilet, numbering six:

1. Begin by entering the toilet with the left leg
2. Seek protection and say, "O' Allah truly I ask you to protect me from the filth, dirt, muck, filthiness and from the accursed satan."
3. Clean with three stones, three clay pieces, three handfuls of dust
4. Leaving with the right leg
5. Thanking Allah the Exalted by saying, "All praise is for Allah who freed me from what may harm me and preserved in me what benefits me."

    It is narrated that the Prophet (may Allah bestow upon him peace and blessings) said, *"Your forgiveness. Your pardon."*[1] Or in another narration, *"Your pardon, Lord, to you is the journeying."*[2]

    It is narrated that Ali Ibn Abu Talib[3] (may Allah be pleased with him) said, "All praise is for Allah, who preserved me from harm."

6. Not to talk in the toilet, using this as evidence: Abu Bakr As-Saddiq[1] (may Allah be pleased with him) used

---

[1] Abu Dawood, Hakim and Ibn Khuzaymah from Aishah.

[2] Hakim and Ibn Khuzaymah from Aishah.

[3] Ali Ibn Abu Talib was the cousin of the Prophet (may Allah bestow upon him peace and blessings), according to some of the scholars, he was the first Muslim. The Prophet (may Allah bestow upon him peace and blessings) said, "You are my brother in the world and in Heaven." He passed away on the 19th of Ramadan, in the 40th Hijri year. (Isad Al-Ghabah).

to put his cloak on the floor and say, "Oh you, guardian angels, sit here and wait because Allah has told me not to speak in the toilet."[1]

---

[1] Abduallah Ibn Uthman Ibn Amir Al-Qurashi Al-Tammi, known as Abu Bakr. He was a companion of the Prophet (may Allah bestow upon him peace and blessings) before the Prophet hood, followed him into the faith, stayed with him in Mecca and emigrated with him. He is the father of Aishah (Mother of the Believers). He passed on Friday on the 13 Hijri. (Isad Al-Ghabah).

25. Chapter on the description of ablution

If a person wishes to do ablution, he washes his hands three times then says, "By your great name Allah, All praise is yours for the religion of Islam." Before uncovering your nakedness and doing Istinja, and after completing Istinja say, "O' Allah, make me amongst the oft turning to you and purified. And make me amongst the sincere worshippers and those who are not fearful or sad." Or in another narration, "All praise is for Allah who sends pure water from the skies and makes Islam a light, guiding, proof for His Heavens, to His blessed paradise, to the abode of peace. "O' Allah, protect my private place and forgive my sins whilst I uncover my nakedness."

Then use Miswak, if you have it, otherwise it is permissible to use your finger. Say, "O' Allah, enlighten my heart, fragrance my breath and forgive my sins."

Then rinse and say, "O' Allah, help me to recite your remembrance, thank You and perfect my worship to You." Clean out your nose and say, "O' Allah, allow me to smell the fragrance of Heaven and provide me blessing from therein. And prevent me from smelling the stench of hell; whilst you are pleased with me." Then wash your face and say, "O Allah, enlighten my face on a day when you enlighten the faces of your people. And do not darken my face on a day you will darken the faces of your enemies." Or in another narration, "O Allah, enlighten my face, purify my heart and expand my chest."

Wash your right hand and say, "O' Allah, please give my book into my right hand and reckon me, an easy reckoning."[1]

Wash your left hand and say, "O' Allah, please do not give my book into my left hand nor behind my back or make my reckoning difficult."

Wipe your head and say, "O' Allah, envelop me in Your mercy, send blessings upon me, free me from my sins. Shade me under Your throne on a day when there will be no shade except Yours."

Wipe your ears and say, **"O' Allah make me of those who hear advice and follow the best thereof."[2]**

Wipe your neck and say, "O' Allah free my neck from the fire and protect me from the neck brace, handcuffs and shackles."

Then wash your right foot and say, "O' Allah affirm my feet upon the traverse; on a day that feet will slip." Or in another narration, "The day when the feet will tremble."

Wash your left foot and say, "O' Allah make my works gratitude, my sins forgiven, my works acceptable and my business not devoid of your pardon. O' Almighty, O' Forgiver, by Your mercy; O' Most Merciful of those who show mercy."

When you have finished ablution it is recommended for you to look to the Heavens and say, ("All praise is for Allah upon

---

[1] A supplication referring to the reckoning/Hisab on the day of judgement.

[2] Quran the Troops 39.17-18.

completing ablution and following the Sunna"). Then say, "Your glory and praise O Allah; I testify that there is no deity except You alone; You have no partner; I seek forgiveness and repent to You." Then look to the earth and say, "I testify that Muhammad is your Prophet and Messenger." Then recite Sura the Power "**Lo! We revealed it on the night of power**"[1] once after ablution. Whoever reads it once, Allah writes for him fifty years of fasting during the day and praying during the night." If read twice, Allah gives them what he gave the bosom friend[2], the speech[3], the raised[4] and the Beloved.[5] Whoever reads it three times, Allah opens eight doors of heaven for him, and he enters from whichever door he wishes without reckoning or punishment.

Abu Hurayrah (may Allah be pleased with him) narrated that the Prophet (may Allah bestow upon him peace and blessings) said, "Whoever reads Sura "the Power"[6] after ablution, once, Allah records him amongst the truthful ones. Whoever reads it twice, Allah records him amongst the martyrs and the sincere. Whoever reads it three times, Allah (Mighty and Majestic) gathers them up amongst the Prophets, upon them peace, on the Day of Judgement."[7]

---

[1] Quran: the Power 96:1.
[2] The Prophet Ibrahim/Abraham –upon him peace.
[3] The Prophet Musa/Moses – upon him peace.
[4] The Prophet Isa/Jesus – upon him peace or the Prophet Idriss – upon him peace.
[5] The Prophet Muhammad (peace and blessings of Allah be upon him).
[6] Quran: The Power 96.1.
[7] Ad-Daylami in Firdaws Al-Khitab but this hadith is **very weak!**

26. Chapter on the kinds of purification

Know that purification is of six kinds:

1. To clean your heart from everything except Allah
2. To clean your heart from rancour, deception, slander and envy
3. To clean your tongue from lies, backbiting and tale-bearing
4. To clean your body from prohibited food and alcohol
5. Clean your external from prohibited dress
6. Purify yourself lawfully until you are able to pray.

Hassan Ibn Ziad[1] narrated that Abu Hanifa said, "Perform ablution with three ritals[2] of water: one for Istinja, one for all your limbs except your feet and one for your feet. And if you need more you can do so."

---

[1] Al-Hassan Ibn Zaid Al-Lulu was a student of Muhammad Ibn Sam'at, Muhammad Ibn Shaja'a Al-Talji and others. Ahmed Ibn Abdulhamid Al-Thari said, "I have not seen anyone with better character than Al-Hassan Ibn Zaid." He never refused a request and was easy to be with. He was noted for his understanding, knowledge, abstinence and piety. If there was not a transcript in the six books, his narration would be accepted. Taj Al-Tarajim.

[2] A type of container.

27. Chapter on the types of cleanliness

Know that cleanliness is of two types:
1. Actual cleanliness.
2. Legal cleanliness.
Legal cleanliness is ablution; bathing from conjugal relations, periods, post partum bleeding. Actual cleanliness is dry ablution by soil.

28. Chapter on the kinds of Sunna

Know that the Sunna is of two kinds:
1. Sunna, if adopted is guidance, and leaving it is misguidance, like the call to prayer, call to commence, congregation, Witr, two units before Fajr and four units before Zuhur.
2. Taking the Sunna is preferable and leaving it is not objectionable like supererogatory fasts, prayer, alms and so on.

29. Chapter on different issues

Imam Muhammad said in the book of prayer, "When a person desires to pray then they should perform ablution." Qadi Abu Laith said, "We mean that if he is impure then perform ablution." Imam Muhammad mentioned ablution and concealed the section on impurity. He disliked beginning the book of prayer by mentioning impurity because it is a noble book.

Shaqiq Ibn Ibrahim Az-Zahid Al-Balkhi[1] said, "I read the book of prayer to Abu Yusuf in a hat shop. On my head was a hat made of cotton, he said, "O' Abu Ali, I have not seen under the sky or upon the noble green land, a more superior than this book except the Book of Allah the Exalted."

Abu Yusuf said, "I damaged the book of prayer under my sleeve several times and each time I would read I would find some new benefit from it."

Muhammad Ibn Salamah said, "I read the book of prayer and have had it read to me four hundred times; and I did not look at it except that I gained a new benefit from it, every time."

---

[1] Abu Ali. He was a companion of Abu Yusuf, Ibrahim Ibn Adham and a teacher Hatim As-Samm. He was the first to lecture about Tasawwaf thought out of Khurasan. He was very rich and it was said that he owned 300 towns and then he gave them away. He read the Quran twenty times until he could distinguish between the world and the hereafter. "We did not provide you anything except as a pass time in the life of the world and what Allah has is better and everlasting."He died a Martyr in 194 Hijri.

It was asked, "What Sunna replaces the obligation?" Answer, "Wiping the leather socks is Sunna and it replaces an obligation."

It was asked, "Which (major) impurity has no obligation for bathing?" Answer, "Washing from major impurity and leaving one place where water did not reach, so he can wash that place and not all the other limbs."

It was asked, "Which prayer is permissible to pray without recitation?" Answer, "Illiterate, dumb, late-comer and the deaf."

It was asked, "Which obligation, if performed Allah will not accept, and if not performed they will be rewarded." Answer, "From the menstruating female or the post-partum bleeding female; no prayer or fast are acceptable from them but they are rewarded if left."[1]

It was asked, "How do we know the obligation from the Sunna, and the Sunna from the supererogatory?" Answer, "Obligations are what Allah ordered and the Prophet (may Allah bestow upon him peace and blessings) did and did not leave during his life, this is obligatory.

As for what the Prophet (may Allah bestow upon him peace and blessings) did himself, and was described as such, for his entire life, this is Sunna.

---

[1] She is rewarded for the prayers that she misses but must make up the missed fasts of Ramadan.

As for the supererogatory, what the Prophet (may Allah bestow upon him peace and blessings) did sometimes and mentioned its benefits to his nation, then this became supererogatory for us.

Other questions: a pillar (definition): If left a person is a sinner and if rejected is non-Muslim. Sunna[1]: If left then he is a sinner and rejection is heresy. Nafal: If left a person is a transgressor and if rejected heresy, but increases in degrees if done, and if left he falls in degrees.

It was asked, "Is purification needed for prayer or because of impurity?" Answer, "Purification is necessary because of prayer if minor filth is present. When a prayer time enters and he is in a state of purity, then there is no ablution to be performed. And if the prayer time enters and he is impure, then ablution is upon him."

"Is it obligatory to testify faith or is it Sunna?" Answer, "Faith is confirmation on the tongue, of the unity of Allah the Exalted and the belief in the Chosen[2] (may Allah bestow upon him peace and blessings). He was sent with what the Prophets (upon them all peace) came with, sending prayers and greetings upon them is necessary. Repeating and making it habitual is Sunna.

---

[1] Sunna here must be referring to Wajib actions and the Nafal must be referring to the Sunna actions.

[2] One of the names of the Prophet Muhammad (may Allah bestow peace and blessings upon him).

"How do we know Allah?" Say, "We do not know Him by specifics, rather we know him how as He described Himself. He described himself until we knew Him."

"What are faith, Islam and excellence/Ihsan?" Answer, "Faith is affirmation on the tongue (belief in the heart) and the parts of the body. Islam is obeying His orders (The Exalted) and avoiding the prohibitions. Excellence/Ihsan is being good to the creation of Allah the Exalted and sympathy for the weak without haughtiness." And Ihsan is to pray to Allah as if you see Him; although you cannot see Him; but He sees you.[1]

Az-Zahid Shaqiq Al-Balkhi was asked about faith, Marifah, Tawheed, Sacred Law and religion. He said, "Faith is confirming the unity of Allah the Exalted without asking how and comparing. Marifah/Gnosis is knowledge of Allah the Exalted without asking how and without comparing. Tawheed/Unity of God[2] is the servant affirming that Allah is One,[3] without partner, sincerely without comparison or denial. Sacred Law is to obey your Lord, performing the orders and avoiding the prohibitions. Religion is persisting and affirming these four until death."

Know that faith: Islam, Sacred Law, and religion have twenty aspects. Five in the heart, five on the tongue, five that the limbs do and five outside the limbs.

---

[1] Bukhari and Muslim from Umar (part of the Hadith Gibril).
[2] Meaning God/Allah is One.
[3] Abu Hanifa in Fiqh Al-Akbar mentions that Allah/God is one but this is not in a numerical sense. Numbers in Arabic begin with two.

The five that are in the heart: Realise that Allah the Exalted is One and there is no second, He is the Creator of creation, He provides for us and preserves us from state to state.

The five of the tongue are: to believe in Allah the Exalted, His angels, His Messengers, the last day, and that decree, good and bad, are from Allah the Exalted.

The five aspects that are of the limbs are: fasting, prayer, Hajj, Zakah and ablution, (bathing from partner relations, periods, post partum bleeding etc).

The five that are outside the limbs are: obeying the ruler, sultan, Imam, the caller of prayer, wiping over leather socks and the prayer of the two Eids.

Question, "If it is asked, was faith created or uncreated?" We say, "Affirming faith, following guidance, and the follow up works of the servant, are created. The Lord has placed guidance but it is not created and who says guidance is created is a disbeliever."

The book, Initiation by the Jurist Abu Laith, is now complete and all praise is due for Allah and may salutations and benedictions endlessly fall upon his final Messenger Muhammad (may Allah bestow upon him peace and blessings).